Apes & Monkeys

PHOTOS AND FACTS FOR EVERYONE

BY ISIS GAILLARD

Learn With Facts Series

Book 2

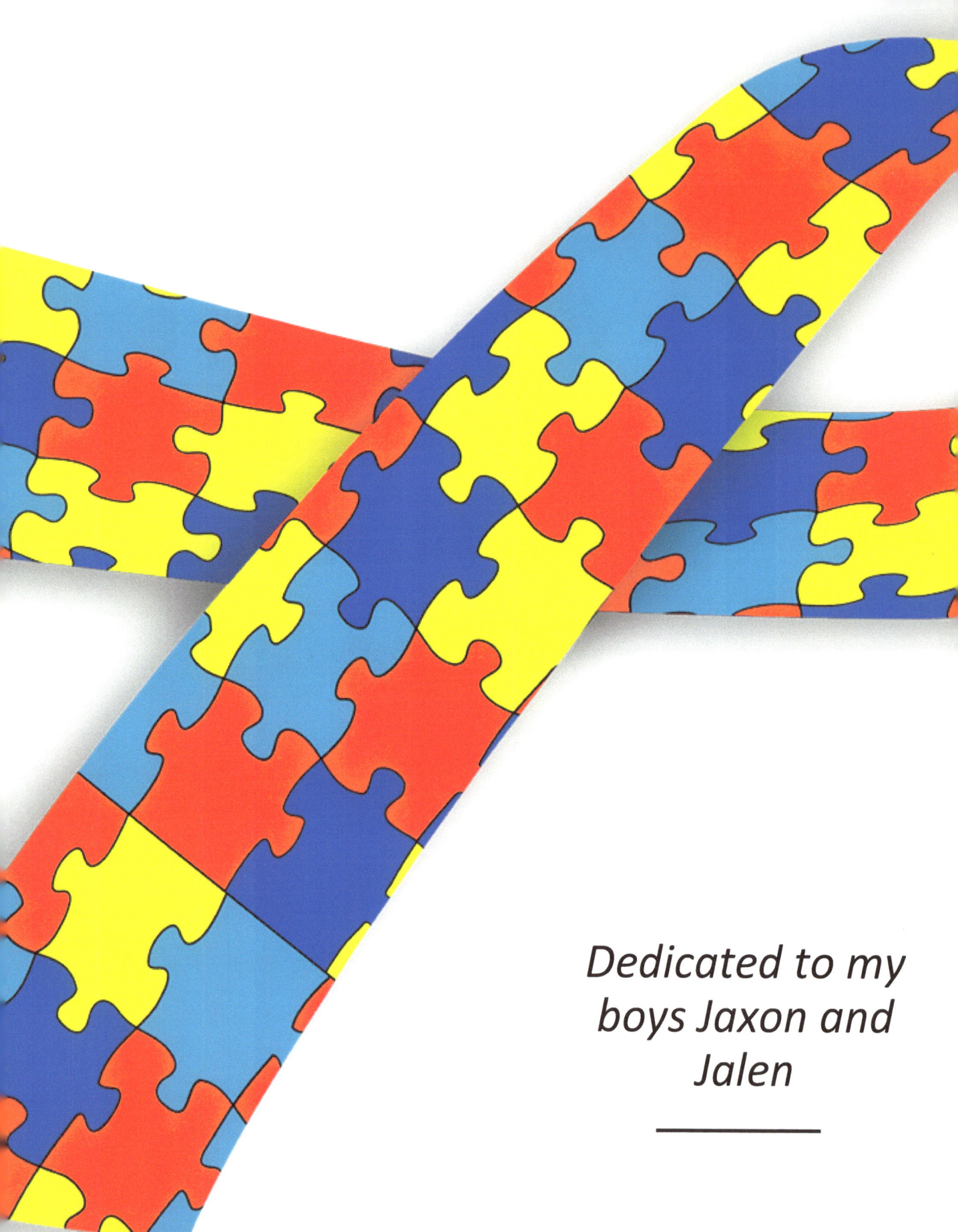

Dedicated to my boys Jaxon and Jalen

_____

CONTENTS

Image Credits: Royalty-free images reproduced under license from various stock image repositories.

Isis Gaillard. Apes and Monkeys: Photos and Facts for Everyone (Learn With Facts Series Book 2). Ebook Edition.
Learn With Facts an imprint of TLM Media LLC

eISBN: 978-1-63497-129-4
ISBN-13: 978-1-63497-251-2

Introduction

Apes are old-world anthropoid, well-evolved creatures, particularly a clade of tailless catarrhine primates: their natural superfamily Hominoidea are primates and class Mammalia. People confuse apes with monkeys; however, they are entirely two diverse species. Unlike monkeys, apes are far bigger than monkeys, and they don't have tails.

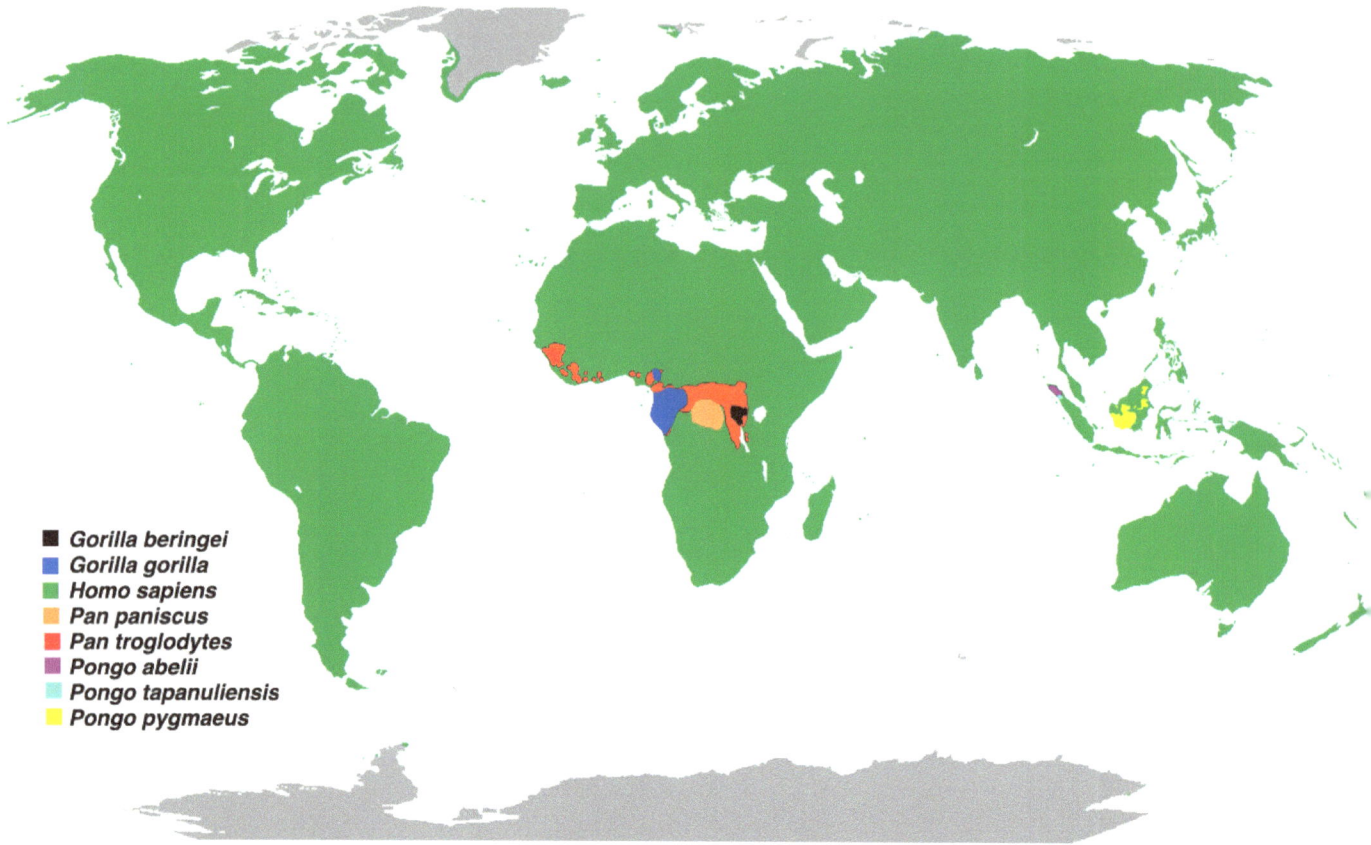

Gorilla beringei
Gorilla gorilla
Homo sapiens
Pan paniscus
Pan troglodytes
Pongo abelii
Pongo tapanuliensis
Pongo pygmaeus

The apes are local to Africa and Southeast Asia. Apes are the biggest primates, and the orangutan, a type of ape, is the biggest living arboreal animal. At the same time, monkeys tend to settle on the tropical rainforests of Africa, Central America, South America, and Asia.

Most monkeys are so decently adjusted to living in rainforest overhangs pulverization of this territory is wrecking to their numbers.

Description

There are four types of apes. These are the gorillas, orangutans, chimpanzees, and gibbons

1. Gorillas

Gorillas are the biggest of the extraordinary apes. The male gorilla figure is 5.6 ft and 400 lb. On the other hand, female gorillas' stature is 4.6 ft, and their weight is 200 lb.

There are two sorts of gorillas: Eastern gorillas and Western gorillas. They are discovered in diverse parts of Africa like Angola, Burundi (reports conceivably wiped out), Cameroon, Central African Republic, Congo, the Democratic Republic of the Congo, Guinea, Nigeria, Rwanda, and Uganda.

Western Gorillas are further ordered into two sorts western swamp gorillas and cross-stream gorillas.

2. Orangutans

Orangutans are discovered in Asia, on the islands of Borneo and Sumatra. There are two species: Bornean orangutan and Pongo pygmaeus.

3. Chimpanzees

Chimpanzees are discovered in Africa and have the biggest go of any African ape. They extend from Senegal in the west to Tanzania in the east. There is one type of chimpanzee, Pan troglodytes, and numerous subspecies.

4. Gibbons

Gibbons are discovered in India, Bangladesh, Myanmar, Thailand, Malaysia, Brunei, Indonesia, Cambodia, Laos, Vietnam, and China. There are 16 species in four genera: Hylobates, Hoolock, Symphalangus, and Nomascus in gibbons. Male gibbons are bigger than females. Males are around the range of 3 ft long and weigh around the range of 15 pounds.

Monkeys

Monkeys are presumably near the most well-known and enthralling animals on the planet. A monkey is a primate of the Haplorrhini suborder and simian infra order. They are either an old-world monkey or a new-world monkey. There are in the vicinity of 260 known living types of monkeys.

There are diverse monkey species. The new planet monkeys (platyrrhines) are modest to medium-measured. They have wide round nostrils and long tails, prehensile or semi-prehensile. They don't have cheek pockets and cheek cushions.

New world monkey are discovered from South Mexico to midway South America. There are something like 53 types of New World monkeys.

1. Spider monkey

The Spider monkey has extremely long appendages and prehensile tails, resembling a creepy-crawly. While strolling, the monkeys bring their arms above their head.

2. Capuchin monkey

Capuchin monkeys occupy Central and South America. There are some sorts of Capuchin monkeys: white-throated, dark topped, cinnamon, and weeper.

Old World monkey: The Old World monkeys of Africa and Asia involve more or less 132 species in the family Cercopithecidae. They display striking differing qualities in living space, circulation, diet, and social conduct. They are diurnal, bigger than the new planet monkeys, and have diverse physical characteristics.

1. Vervet Monkey

Vervet is an old world monkey that exists in South and East Africa. The skin on their front side is cream shaded when born and it turns dark when they achieve the age of six months.

2. Macaques monkey

Macaques are vast and compelling animals possessing southern Asia. Certain assortments of macaques are the Japanese macaque, the Barbary primate, and the Rhesus macaque.

Size

Smallest monkey on the planet:

Dwarf marmoset is the littlest monkey on the planet, and its physique length runs from 14 to 16 centimeters. Males weigh around 140 grams, and females just 120 grams.

Biggest monkey on the planet:

Mandrill is the biggest monkey on the planet. It is not just the greatest and yet the tallest monkey, moreover, with a shoulder stature of over 50 cm. Its weight is around 50 kg.

Mandrills are discovered in the tropical rainforests and once in a while woodlands of southern Cameroon, Gabon, , exhibition woods beside savanna and its mosaics.

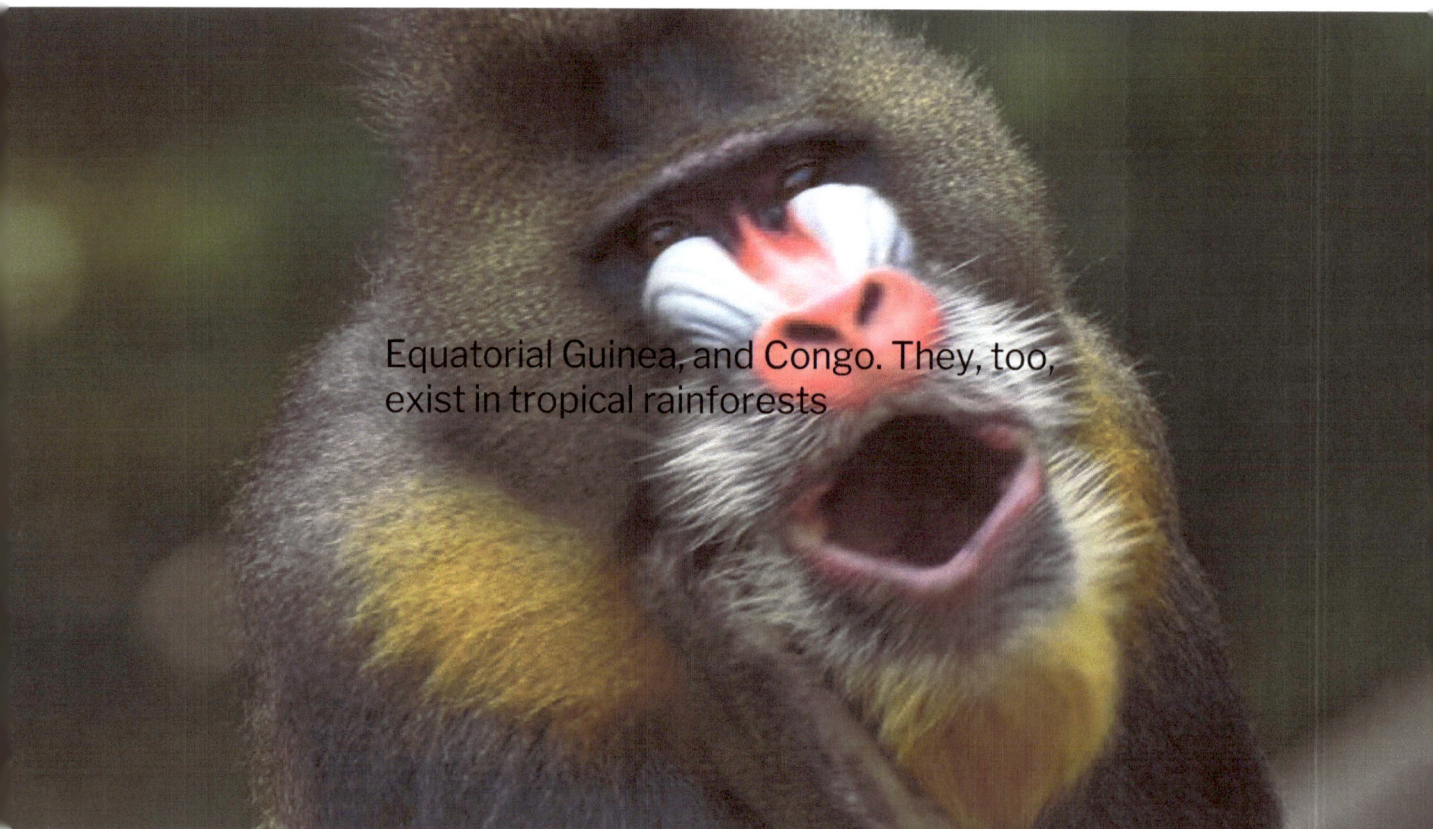

Equatorial Guinea, and Congo. They, too, exist in tropical rainforests

Breeding

Monkeys can breed whenever of the year, as a principle. Females regularly conceive a solitary infant at once. The incubation period goes from 4 to 8 months, hinging on the monkey sort. The infant monkeys are entirely trustworthy for their mothers for nourishment and security. They feast upon their mother's drain for a period from a couple of weeks to two years.

For example, the Black Spider Monkey is noticeably moderate to develop. It begins rearing when it achieves the age of 5 years of age. The single infant monkey is conceived around 20 weeks after mating. The infant monkey sticks tightly to its mother's mid-region for its first four months of life. The point when the toddler monkey gets a bit more senior, it rides on the mother's back, wrapping its tail around her tail for security explanations.

Eating Habit

Gibbons eat fruit primarily but also consume flowers, seeds, and leaves.

Chimpanzees mainly eat fruit and flowers, seeds, and other plant parts. Some groups regularly hunt and consume meat.

Gorillas primarily consume leaves, stems, and roots.

Orangutans also eat fruit, including seeds, leaf shoots, insects, flowers, and bark.

Eating Habit

Monkeys' territories hold an assortment of nourishment sources simultaneously. Even though most monkeys make due on soil-grown foods, seeds, and abandons, they are likewise shrewd eaters, feasting on creepy crawlies, little warm-blooded creatures, eggs, and reptiles if given the possibility.

Much of a monkey's eating regimen is managed by nature's turf in which it exists. Monkeys acclimate for the trees will consume more foods grown from the ground, while monkeys on the open savanna will be more rapacious as a rule.

Interesting Facts

TOP 10 WEIRDEST MONKEYS ON EARTH

1. Tarsier: These are altogether different from other monkeys as they are flesh-eating animals nourishing bugs, reptiles, and even winged creatures. They are exceptionally forceful monkeys and engaged enough to find the flying bugs and fowls. They are dependably switched on ambushing mode. Tarsiers are engaged communicators and can impart at exceptionally level frequencies.

2. Probosci's Monkey: These monkeys are local to Asia and recognized as a vast assembly of monkey crew. It is a fascinating reality that sexual dimorphism exists in this kind.

3. Douc Langur: These are primarily found in South East Asia. This monkey is also listed as the endangered species of South East Asia.

4. Golden Snub Nose Monkey: These are smaller and cat-like monkeys. The face has no hairs and is distinguished from the rest of the body. These are active and form groups of 10-15 individuals.

5. Gelada Baboon: Gelada baboons are large primate monkeys having distinct physical features. These are also called breast apes.

6. Saki Monkey: These are native to South America. The face has off-white to yellow marks, and the rest of the coat is monochromatic.

7. Red Uakari Monkey: This South American fellow has a characteristic red face, due to which they are called red uakari monkeys.

8. Orangutan: Orangutans mainly belong to Asian origins. The life duration of female monkeys is longer than that of males.

9. Mustached Guenon: This monkey is also native to African countries. These are mainly famous due to their movements.

10. De Brazza's Monkey: This old-world monkey is native to Africa. Life span ranges from 25 to 30 years, and in rare cases, it may live up to 40 years.

THE END

Thanks for reading facts about Apes & Monkeys. I am a parent of two boys on the autism spectrum. I am always advocating for Autism Spectrum Disorders which part of the proceeds of this book goes to many Non-Profit Autism Organizations. I would love if you would leave a review.

Author Note from Isis Gaillard:

Thanks For Reading! I hope you enjoyed the fact book about **Apes & Monkeys**. Please check out all the Learn With Facts and the Kids Learn With Pictures series available.

Visit **www.IsisGaillard.com** and **www.LearnWithFacts.com** to find more books in the Learn With Facts Series

More Books In The Series

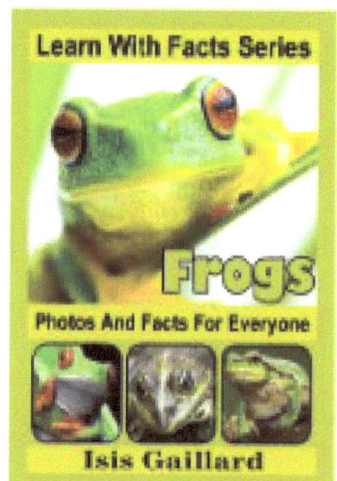

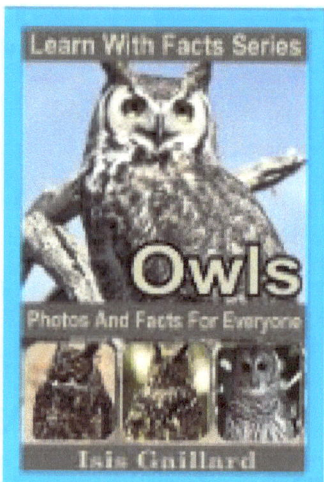

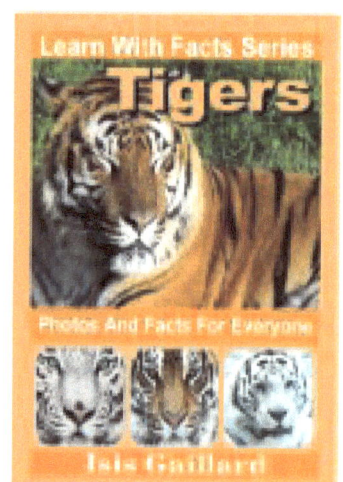

Learn With Facts Series
ALLIGATORS AND CROCODILES
Photos And Facts For Everyone
Isis Gaillard

Learn With Facts Series
BUTTERFLIES
Photos And Facts For Everyone
Isis Gaillard

Learn With Facts Series
Frogs
Photos And Facts For Everyone
Isis Gaillard

Learn With Facts Series
Owls
Photos And Facts For Everyone
Isis Gaillard

Learn With Facts Series
PANDAS
Photos And Facts For Everyone
Isis Gaillard

Learn With Facts Series
Tigers
Photos And Facts For Everyone
Isis Gaillard

Over 75 books in the Learn With Facts Series.

Puzzle 1

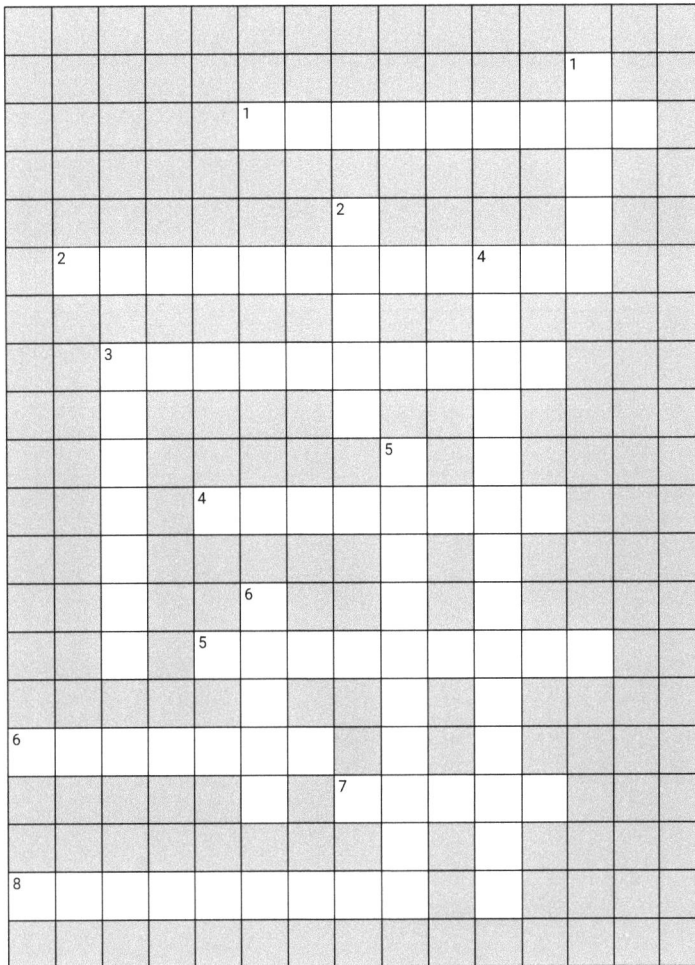

ACROSS
1. Dinosaurs
2. Caterpillars
3. Crocodiles
4. Dolphins
5. Hedgehogs
6. Beavers
7. Foxes
8. Elephants

DOWN
1. Frogs
2. Birds
3. Cougars
4. Apes and Monkeys
5. Chameleons
6. Bears

Puzzle 2

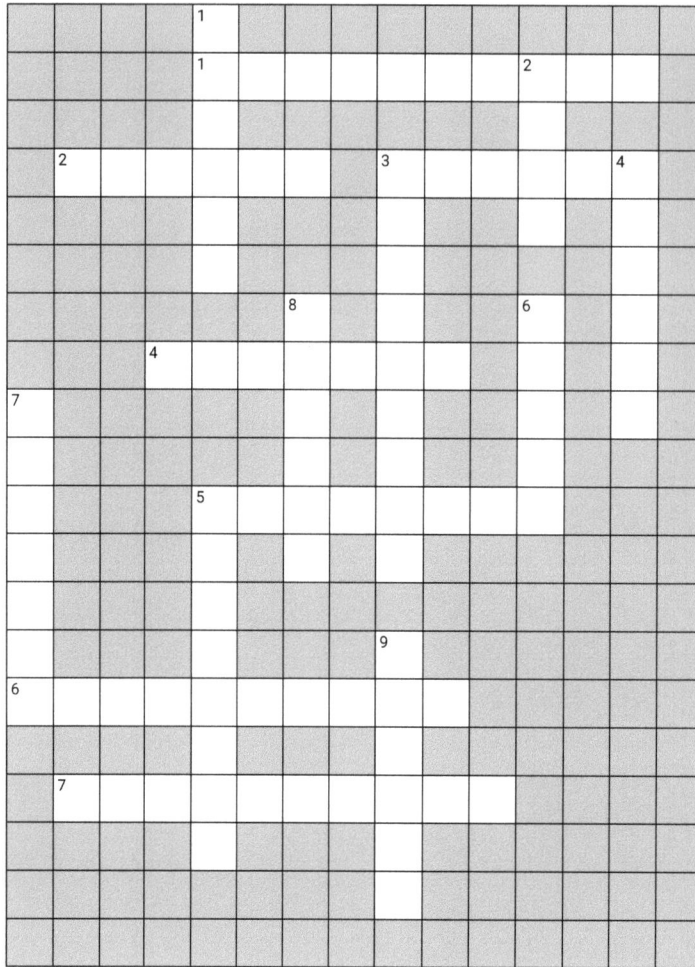

ACROSS
1. Alligators
2. Tigers
3. Koalas
4. Alpacas
5. Peacocks
6. Sea Turtles
7. Rhinoceros

DOWN
1. Camels
2. Owls
3. Kangaroos
4. Snakes
5. Penguins
6. Lions
7. Spiders
8. Pandas
9. Zebras

Puzzle 3

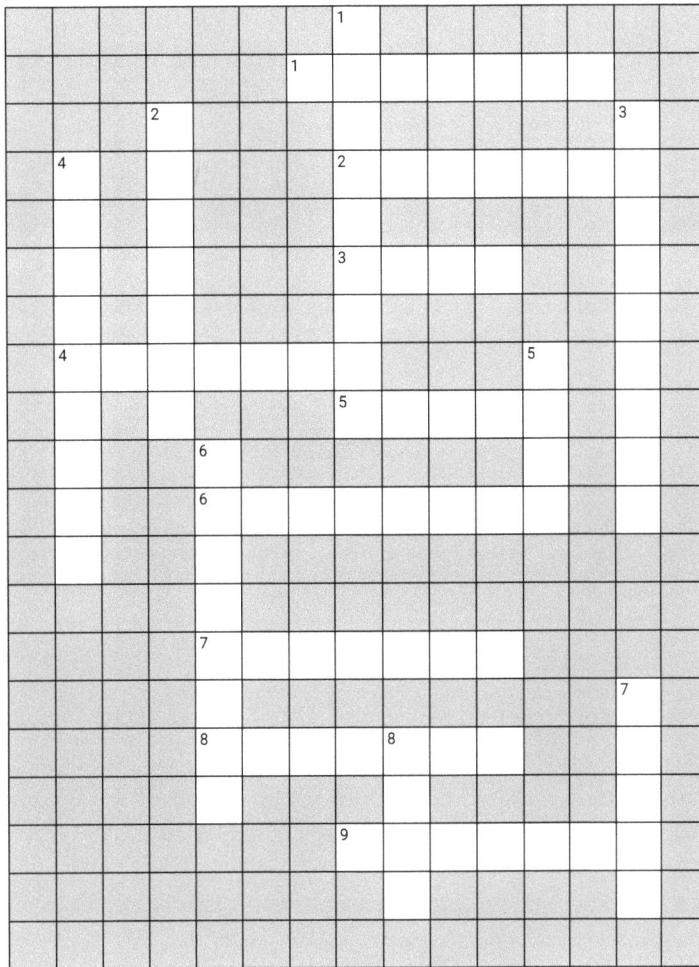

ACROSS
1. Meerkat
2. Lizards
3. Fish
4. Parrots
5. Hyena
6. Leopards
7. Iguanas
8. Gazelle
9. Insects

DOWN
1. Jellyfish
2. Jaguars
3. Ostriches
4. Octopuses
5. Bats
6. Flamingo
7. Moose
8. Lynx

Puzzle 4

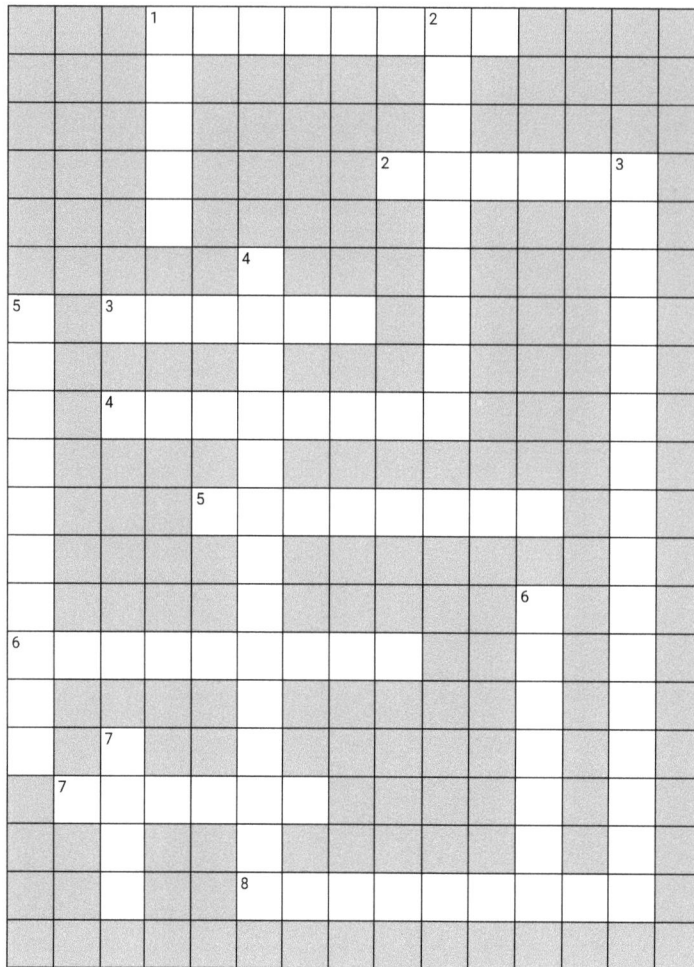

ACROSS
1. Starfish
2. Whales
3. Ponies
4. Roosters
5. Anteater
6. Armadillo
7. Wolves
8. Scorpions

DOWN
1. Swans
2. Seahorses
3. Seals and Sea Lions
4. Pigs and Piglets
5. Polar Bears
6. Buffalo
7. Cows

Puzzle 5

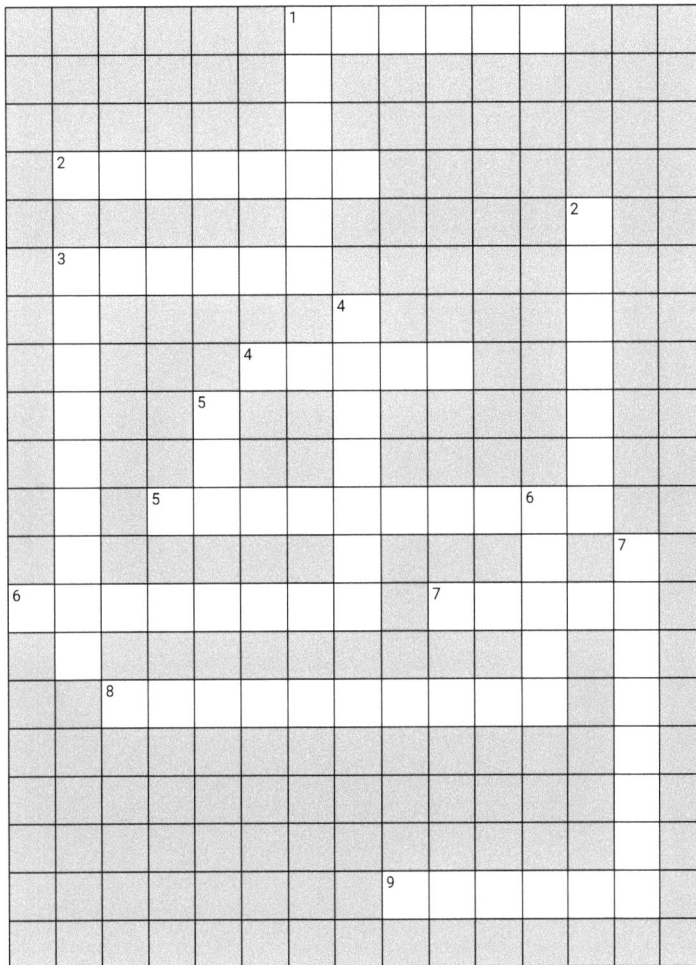

ACROSS
1. Sloths
2. Echidna
3. Storks
4. Sheep
5. Guinea Pigs
6. Platypus
7. Llama
8. Porcupines
9. Sharks

DOWN
1. Skunks
2. Donkeys
3. Squirrels
4. Ferrets
5. Emu
6. Goats
7. Raccoons

Puzzle 6

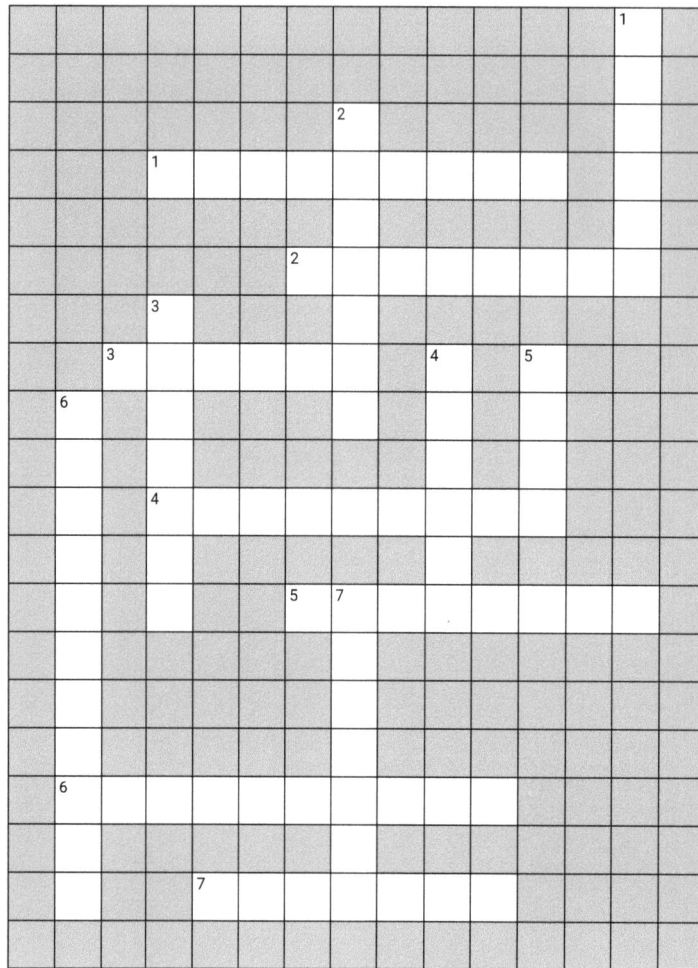

ACROSS
1. Tortoises
2. Gorillas
3. Cattle
4. Aardvarks
5. Opossums
6. Amphibians
7. Weasels

DOWN
1. Lemurs
2. Coyotes
3. Mammals
4. Walrus
5. Yaks
6. Farm Animals
7. Puffins

Puzzle 1

```
                              ¹F
            ¹D I N O S A U R S  O
                  ²B           G
²C A T E R P I L L ⁴A R S
                  R        P
  ³C R O C O D I L E S
  O              S        S
  U           ⁵C        A
  G ⁴D O L P H I N S
  A              A        D
  R      ⁶B     M        M
  S  ⁵H E D G E H O G S
            A        L     N
⁶B E A V E R S      E     K
            S  ⁷F O X E S
                  N     Y
⁸E L E P H A N T S      S
```

Puzzle 2

```
            ¹C
            ¹A L L I G A T ²O R S
            M              W
³T I G E R S      ³K O A L A ⁴S
            L        A        N
            S        N        A
                  ⁸P  G     ⁶L  K
            ⁴A L P A C A S  I  E
⁷S              N     R     O  S
P              D     O     N
I           ⁵P E A C O C K S
D           E     S     S
E           N
R           G        ⁹Z
⁶S E A T U R T L E S
            I        B
  ⁷R H I N O C E R O S
            S        A
                  S
```

Puzzle 3

```
                        ¹J
                  ¹M E E R K A T
         ²J        L              ³O
⁴O     A        ²L I Z A R D S     S
C     G        Y              T
T     U        ³F I S H        R
O     A        I              I
²P A R R O T S        ⁵B        C
U     S        ⁵H Y E N A      H
S        ⁶F              T     E
E        ⁶L E O P A R D S     S
S        A
         M
         ⁷I G U A N A S
         N              ⁷M
         ⁸G A Z E ⁸L L E      O
         O        Y        O
              ⁹I N S E C T S
              X        E
```

Puzzle 4

```
         ¹S T A R F I ²S H
         W        E
         A        A
         N     ²W H A L E ³S
         S        O     E
            ⁴P     R     A
⁵P ³P O N I E S   S     L
O        O     G        S
L ⁴R O O S T E R S     A
A        A           N
R     ⁵A N T E A T E R  D
B        D           S
E        P        ⁶B  E
⁶A R M A D I L L O  U  A
R        G        F  L
S  ⁷C     L        F  I
⁷W O L V E S      A  O
   W     T        L  N
   S  ⁸S C O R P I O N S
```

Puzzle 5

Across:
- SLOTHS
- ECHIDNA
- STORKS
- SHEEP
- GUINEA PIGS
- PLATYPUS
- LLAMA
- PORCUPINES
- SHARKS

Down (letters visible): SKUNK, DONKEY, SQUIRRELPS, EMM, FERRETS, GOOSOON, RACCOON

Puzzle 6

Across:
- TORTOISES
- GORILLAS
- CATTLE
- AARDVARKS
- OPOSSUMS
- AMPHIBIANS
- WEASELS

Down (letters visible): LEMUR, COYOTE, MMMALS, WASLU, YAK, FARMANIMALS, PUFFINS

Set 1

```
A  L  L  X  R  F  K  Y  S  A  S  I  X  K  P
S  Q  H  Y  N  O  W  O  G  R  B  G  S  O  W
E  L  X  D  B  X  O  B  A  I  A  D  O  R  R
L  G  W  B  Z  E  U  Y  T  L  R  G  F  R  D
E  K  G  O  O  S  B  X  Z  I  A  V  U  U  F
P  L  D  W  H  I  E  H  B  E  I  S  Y  O  S
H  S  D  V  I  C  E  C  T  E  Y  W  C  H  C
A  C  H  I  N  C  H  I  L  L  A  S  A  I  J
N  S  S  B  N  N  F  A  F  J  L  T  Y  A  L
T  O  E  U  T  O  F  P  M  V  E  D  C  I  S
S  O  D  S  M  F  S  V  T  E  R  S  O  W  R
E  R  Z  O  R  A  G  A  H  Y  L  N  Q  V  A
A  A  F  E  L  O  T  C  U  I  S  E  Q  Y  E
G  G  Q  R  G  P  H  O  K  R  A  K  O  L  B
L  N  T  C  X  X  H  Z  P  F  S  E  A  N  B
E  A  L  I  S  E  L  I  D  O  C  O  R  C  S
S  K  D  E  K  V  W  S  N  D  P  N  D  Z  I
S  G  O  H  E  G  D  E  H  S  O  P  F  G  I
F  H  S  R  E  V  A  E  B  P  C  C  I  B  S
A  H  B  P  E  G  I  R  A  F  F  E  S  H  E
```

Word List

Bears
Beavers
Birds
Chameleons
Cheetahs
Chinchillas
Cougars
Crocodiles
Dinosaurs

Dolphins
Eagles
Elephants
Foxes
Frogs
Giraffes
Hedgehogs
Hippopotamus
Horses

Kangaroos
Koalas
Lions
Owls

Set 2

```
Z  G  K  M  V  B  E  E  S  S  O  V  E  E  P
P  E  A  C  O  C  K  S  F  R  A  N  E  Y  H
G  I  P  Z  A  L  L  I  G  A  T  O  R  S  B
C  J  G  A  E  N  F  V  S  U  U  L  Y  C  R
Y  R  R  U  N  L  X  Z  R  G  Q  K  C  S  C
H  S  I  F  A  D  L  Y  E  A  N  O  E  I  K
R  P  C  D  H  N  A  E  G  J  T  I  P  H  S
H  I  F  A  N  W  A  S  I  X  P  O  X  N  S
I  D  Z  A  M  A  P  S  T  P  Q  I  E  A  Y
N  E  F  L  H  E  S  B  U  X  T  T  R  G  H
O  R  L  P  G  M  L  P  T  O  T  B  B  S  S
C  S  A  A  U  M  D  S  A  I  E  A  L  E  I
E  A  M  C  E  N  W  S  K  Z  T  C  R  A  F
R  A  I  A  A  U  N  D  M  S  R  T  W  T  Y
O  L  N  S  S  I  N  K  S  E  F  F  V  U  L
S  J  G  Z  U  A  V  E  N  R  R  T  K  R  L
G  O  O  G  S  O  C  B  A  H  S  I  A  T  E
D  I  N  T  F  C  B  Y  K  Q  Z  C  B  L  J
B  E  A  Q  B  U  T  T  E  R  F  L  I  E  S
P  C  I  N  S  E  C  T  S  E  V  Q  K  S  Z
```

Word List

Alligators	Flamingo	Penguins
Alpacas	Gazelle	Rhinoceros
Bats	Hyena	Sea Turtles
Bees	Iguanas	Snakes
Butterflies	Insects	Spiders
Camels	Jaguars	Tigers
Cats and Kittens	Jellyfish	Zebras
Dogs and Puppies	Pandas	
Fish	Peacocks	

Set 3

P	S	G	U	K	P	O	N	I	E	S	C	M	M	S
O	A	N	S	O	C	T	O	P	U	S	E	S	I	E
T	T	R	O	E	R	O	O	S	T	E	R	S	Q	A
C	S	K	R	I	F	K	K	J	M	Y	P	W	S	L
M	Y	J	A	O	P	O	V	J	L	C	I	A	G	S
W	K	C	Q	E	T	R	W	E	S	U	G	N	G	A
H	Z	E	F	I	Y	S	O	R	A	V	S	S	O	N
W	O	L	V	E	S	P	A	C	E	S	A	S	S	D
L	G	Y	Z	W	A	E	S	S	Y	N	W	T	S
V	X	T	L	R	B	D	O	N	D	O	D	N	R	E
H	G	I	D	R	R	O	A	Y	G	S	P	S	I	A
W	E	S	A	A	M	C	G	A	T	T	I	E	C	L
U	H	L	Z	X	I	G	R	P	A	A	G	A	H	I
L	O	I	E	L	T	D	E	K	B	R	L	H	E	O
P	L	O	E	X	O	U	R	I	S	F	E	O	S	N
L	N	P	Q	D	A	E	R	D	G	I	T	R	N	S
B	R	P	O	V	E	S	W	T	X	S	S	S	V	S
A	E	M	L	M	L	Y	N	X	L	H	T	E	W	G
D	O	O	X	X	O	W	H	A	L	E	S	S	H	M
K	V	R	A	N	T	E	A	T	E	R	S	A	J	T

Word List

Anteater
Komodo Dragons
Leopards
Lizards
Lynx
Meerkat
Moose
Octopuses
Ostriches

Parrots
Pelicans
Pigs and Piglets
Polar Bears
Ponies
Roosters
Scorpions
Seahorses
Seals and Sea Lions

Starfish
Swans
Turtles
Whales
Wolves

Set 4

```
Z  P  O  R  C  U  P  I  N  E  S  C  M  F  Z
P  K  N  S  K  C  E  O  Y  U  H  A  O  A  I
E  C  H  I  D  N  A  R  F  M  O  E  U  A  H
K  H  C  K  W  Q  E  E  S  E  R  R  N  K  F
R  M  P  L  S  E  U  K  Y  G  O  A  T  S  X
N  A  R  L  D  Q  R  J  N  E  C  H  A  P  V
S  H  C  N  A  O  U  U  G  B  H  P  I  B  L
T  Y  I  C  T  T  P  I  U  B  I  L  N  B  I
C  E  E  S  O  F  Y  F  R  E  C  T  L  Z  V
R  O  G  K  E  O  F  P  Z  R  K  D  I  S  E
F  D  W  I  N  A  N  L  U  R  E  O  O  L  D
E  W  I  S  L  O  G  S  L  S  N  L  N  O  N
R  E  T  O  V  V  D  X  U  A  S  G  S  T  A
R  C  H  I  P  M  U  N  K  S  M  W  W  H  I
E  W  S  H  A  R  K  S  D  Q  S  A  M  S  N
T  I  D  Y  C  Z  O  O  T  H  O  R  A  D  A
S  Y  T  E  G  U  I  N  E  A  P  I  G  S  M
J  S  E  T  E  S  E  E  R  D  L  O  J  T  S
J  K  H  H  F  R  P  S  K  U  N  K  S  N  A
X  A  R  M  A  D  I  L  L  O  C  E  R  L  T
```

Word List

Armadillo	Ferrets	Sharks
Buffalo	Goats	Sheep
Chickens	Guinea Pigs	Skunks
Chipmunks	Llama	Sloths
Cows	Mountain Lions	Squirrels
Deer	Platypus	Storks
Donkeys	Porcupines	Tasmanian Devil
Echidna	Raccoons	
Emu	Reindeer	

Set 5

```
3  W  M  S  E  S  I  O  T  R  O  T  T  X  M
0  Q  M  A  R  S  U  P  I  A  L  S  S  S  V
D  B  G  Z  R  J  A  D  D  G  V  B  C  E  A
A  A  V  V  H  I  S  L  A  M  M  A  M  T  N
N  S  L  A  M  I  N  A  M  R  A  F  S  O  T
G  B  J  B  K  X  S  E  Y  O  X  R  M  Y  E
E  G  A  E  T  U  X  K  L  P  X  I  U  O  L
R  P  U  M  R  N  C  F  S  I  C  C  S  C  O
O  C  U  L  O  A  O  L  R  B  F  T  S  F  P
U  M  A  F  T  J  E  U  S  V  R  E  O  Y  E
S  W  V  T  F  S  I  R  B  A  E  I  P  A  S
A  C  L  M  A  I  U  U  M  D  P  J  O  A  A
N  E  X  E  I  M  N  P  A  N  T  H  E  R  S
I  M  W  G  E  M  H  S  I  T  I  H  B  D  G
M  X  T  L  P  I  Y  F  B  U  L  T  N  V  R
A  J  A  D  B  G  A  S  Q  R  E  B  C  A  L
L  T  D  I  Y  B  K  N  R  K  S  Q  W  R  B
S  P  A  P  V  O  S  O  J  E  S  W  F  K  D
U  N  V  B  N  O  D  L  G  Y  S  J  V  S  Y
S  J  G  O  R  I  L  L  A  S  A  S  A  E  H
```

Word List

30 Dangerous Animals	Mammals	Walrus
Aardvarks	Marine Life	Weasels
Amphibians	Marsupials	Yaks
Antelopes	Opossums	
Cattle	Panthers	
Coyotes	Puffins	
Farm Animals	Reptiles	
Gorillas	Tortoises	
Lemurs	Turkeys	

Set 1

Set 2

Set 3

Set 4

Set 5

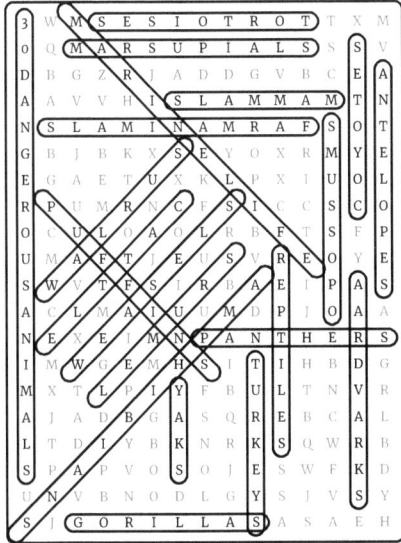

Word search puzzle grid ("30 DANGEROUS ANIMALS"):

3	W	M	S	E	S	I	O	T	R	O	T	T	X	M
0	Q	M	A	R	S	U	P	I	A	L	S	S		V
D	B	G	Z	R	J	A	D	D	G	V	B	C		A
A	A	V	V	H	I	S	L	A	M	M	A	M		N
N	S	L	A	M	I	N	A	M	R	A	F	S		T
G	B	J	B	K	X	S	E	Y	O	X	R	M		E
E	G	A	E	T	U	X	K	L	P	X	I	U		L
R	P	U	M	R	N	C	F	S	I	C	S	S		O
O	C	U	L	O	A	O	L	R	B	F	T	S		P
U	M	A	F	T	I	E	U	S	V	R	E	O		E
S	W	T	F	S	I	R	B	A	A	E	P	Y		S
A	C	L	M	A	I	U	M	D	P	J	Q	A		A
N	E	X	E	I	M	N	P	A	N	T	H	E	R	S
I	M	W	G	E	M	H	S	I	T	I	H	B	D	V
M	X	T	L	P	I	Y	F	B	L	T	N	U	G	R
A	J	A	D	B	G	A	S	Q	R	E	B	C	A	L
L	T	D	I	Y	B	K	N	R	K	S	Q	W	R	B
S	P	A	P	V	O	S	O	J	E	W	F	S	K	B
	N	V	B	N	O	D	L	G	Y	S	J	V	S	H
	J	G	O	R	I	L	L	A	S	A	S	A	E	H

www.ingramcontent.com/pod-product-compliance
Lightning Source LLC
Chambersburg PA
CBHW060825270326
41931CB00002B/63